Grandpa's Lessons on Hiking
and Life

Written by Ruthie Godfrey

Illustrated by Pablo D'Alio

Ruthie Godfrey Books, LLC

FREE TO DOWNLOAD!

Visit RuthieGodfreyBooks.com/FREEBOOK

to get your copy of
Good Deeds Gone Wrong
TODAY!

What folks are saying…

"Sweet story with lessons for all"

"Very relatable and a great conversation starter"

"So sweet with a powerful insight that we sometimes overlook in children"

"Heartwarming!"

"Cute and funny book"

"Great read!"

Dedicated to my sisters --
Sara,
with your infectious enthusiasm,
Beth,
with your steadfast loyalty,
Mary,
with your fierce faith.

I couldn't ask for more amazing women
by my side in navigating
the mountaintops and valleys
of life.

Psalms 19:1
"The heavens declare the glory of God;
the skies proclaim the work of his hands."

Copyright 2020 R.L. Godfrey

Copyright notice: All right reserved under the International and Pan-American Copyright Conventions. No part of this book may be reproduced or transmitted in any form or by any means, electronic or mechanical, including photocopying and recording, or by any information storage and retrieval system, without permission in writing from the publisher.

This is a work of fiction. Names, places, circumstances and incidents are either a product of the author's imagination or are used fictitiously, and any resemblance to any actual persons, living or dead, organizations, events or locales is entirely coincidental.

Warning: the unauthorized reproduction or distribution of this copyrighted work is illegal. Criminal copyright infringement, including infringement without monetary gain, is investigated by the FBI and is punishable by up to five years in prison and a fine of $250,000.

ISBN: (Paperback) 978-1-952402-18-0
ISBN: (Hardcover) 978-1-952402-19-7
ISBN: (Ebook) 978-1-952402-20-3
Library of Congress Control Number: 2021901550

For more information, email: ruthiegodfreybooks@gmail.com www.RuthieGodfreyBooks.com

You sure can learn a lot about
hiking from Grandpa.
And if you pay attention,
you can also learn
a lot about life.

Lesson #1:
Do plenty of research to properly prepare for your adventure.

Lesson #2:
Take time to train.
Build up your strength
for the challenge ahead of you.

Lesson #3:
Make sure
you have the right gear.

Lesson #4:
Fuel yourself
for the long haul.

Lesson #5:
Be friendly on the trail.
Step aside to give space
to the hikers climbing up.

Lesson #6:
Stop to help
fellow hikers in need.

Lesson #7:
Expect the unexpected.

Lesson #8:
Respect nature.
Stay on the path
and pick up after yourself.

Lesson #9:
Pace yourself.
Take the steep climbs
one step at a time.

Lesson #10:
Enjoy the view
and the great perspective
from the mountaintop.

Lesson #11:
Appreciate the growth and the abundance of life in the valleys.

Lesson #12:
Stop to catch your breath and soak in the scenery from time to time.

Lesson #13:
Photos never do justice
to the real thing...
But take lots of photos anyway!

You sure can learn a lot about life from Grandpa. And if you pay attention, you can even learn a lot about hiking, too.

Hiking Tips

Before you head out on any length of hike, there are a few things you ought to consider...

- Check the weather – be sure the conditions will be right for your entire hiking trip.
- Make sure you have the right gear – comfortable hiking shoes, a backpack supplied with snacks, water, and a first aid kit are some of the basics.
- Research the trails – get familiar with your route and what to expect. Make sure the trails are appropriate for your experience and fitness level.
- If you are hiking in high altitude, that means the air is "thinner," and less oxygen is available to your lungs. Be sure to stop to catch your breath as often as needed. And stand upright with your shoulders back to allow your lungs to fully expand.
- Learn the trail etiquette, such as moving to the side of the trail to allow other hikers to pass.

Psalms 19:1 – "The heavens declare the glory of God; the skies proclaim the work of his hands."

FREE TO DOWNLOAD!

Bookmarks in full color
or color them yourself!
Get your bookmarks TODAY at
RuthieGodfreyBooks.com/bookmarks

About the Author

Ruthie Godfrey grew up the youngest of four girls in her family. She had wonderful grandparents who taught her all sorts of things. They taught her to play games, sew, and cook. Most importantly, they taught her to love family.

Ruthie spent many summers hiking with her family. Her dad was an especially avid hiker, and even dedicated years to finding lost hikers on the Search and Rescue team. Ruthie knows that hiking is a wonderful activity that also requires careful preparation!

Ruthie continues to love hiking and her family that has grown bigger over the years. She enjoys walking through beautiful areas of nature. She also loves teaching elementary school. And she loves reading, writing, learning, and growing.

About the Illustrator

Pablo D'Alio is from Buenos Aires, Argentina. He has been drawing since he was 5 years old. At that time, his dad painted portraits. Pablo sat next to him to draw his own things. Eventually, he started stacking sheets of paper to create his own comics. From that moment on, he never stopped drawing, and that is why he made it his career. It was not easy, but now he gets to work doing what he loves every day!

Made in the USA
Columbia, SC
30 June 2025